INDEX

Acknowledgement

I would like to express my sincere gratitude to all those who have supported me throughout the writing of this book. First and foremost, I would like to thank my family for their unwavering encouragement and support. Their love and patience have been the foundation of my success.

I would also like to thank my editor for her invaluable guidance, feedback, and encouragement throughout the writing process. Her insightful comments and suggestions have greatly improved the quality of this work.I am deeply grateful to my friends and colleagues who have provided me with their support and inspiration. Their feedback and constructive criticism have helped me to refine my ideas and strengthen my arguments.

Finally, I would like to express my appreciation to the many scholars whose work has influenced and informed this book. Without their groundbreaking research and insights, this work would not have been possible."Please feel free to modify and personalize this acknowledgement to fit your specific circumstances and the individuals who have contributed to your book.

Experiment No. 1

Aim: To calculate the efficiency of steam distillation.

Equipment Required: Steam distillation assembly

Material Required: distillation flask, condenser, nitrobenzene, and beaker, thermometer, bent Tubes, weighing balance, porcelain chips, separating funnel, sodium chloride, water and Rubber tubing.

Procedure:

1. . Measure 50 ml of nitrobenzene and water mixture and place them in distillation flask.
2. Close the flask with two holed rubber cork and insert thermometer in one hole.
3. Through the other hole, put a bent tube so that steam could pass into distillation flask. Ensure bent tube reaches the bottom of the flask but not touch it.
4. Allow the steam to pass through distillation flask to the condenser.
5. . When thermometer shows constant temperature, collect distillate for 10 minutes in a previously weighed beaker.
6. Determine the weight of the mixture and beaker.
7. Transfer the distillate into a separating funnel and add few grams of sodium chloride. Shake the funnel vigorously till nitrobenzene and water get separated.
8. Collect nitrobenzene separately and weight it.
9. Collect water separately and weight it.

Observations and Calculations:

Molecular weight of nitrobenzene: 123
Molecular weight of water: 18
Weight of beaker = w1 g
Weight of beaker + distillate= w2 g
Weight of beaker and nitrobenzene= w3 g
Weight of nitrobenzene= w3-w1g
Weight of beaker + water= w4 g
Weight of water = w4-w1g
Practical yield= weight of nitrobenzene/ weight of water
Theoretical yield= Molecular weight of nitrobenzene/ molecular weight of water
Percentage efficiency of steam distillation= practical yield / theoretical yield X100

Result: Percentage efficiency of steam distillation was found to be _____%. Precautions: 1. Add porcelain chips to avoid bumping of mixture. 2. Take care not to touch bent tube with the base of flask.

Experiment No. 2

AIM - To determine the overall heat transfer coefficient by heat exchanger.

Equipment Required: Simple distillation assembly, thermometers, and beakers

Procedure:

- Select steam generator, condenser, and bent tube for installation of a simple distillation unit.
- Connect condenser with inlet and outlet pipe for circulation of cold water and connect to tap water. Collect the water used in condensation in a vessel. Measure the volume of water coming out from condenser.
- Place water in flask and heat till steam passes through condenser. Note the temperature of water at entrance.
- Allow the condensation to take place for 15 minutes. e. Collect condensate in a previously weighed beaker. f. Note the temperature of the collected distillate (exit) and volume collected. Calculate average rate of heat transfer and determine overall heat transfer coefficient.

Observations and Calculations:

Weight of condensate (mi)=

Temperature of condensate (tc)=

Weight of outlet water (m2)=

Temperature drop (t1)=ts-tc=

Temperature of water t entrance point (t ent)=

Temperature of water at exit point (t exit)=

Temperature rise Λt= t exit- tent =

Length of the condenser= (l)=

Circumference of the condenser=

T= t2-t1/ 2.303 log ti/t2

Amount of heat lost by steam= q1=m1s1t1m1L

Amount of heat gained by circulating water (q2)= m2s2t2

Average rate of heat transfer Q= q1+q2/2

Overall heat transfer coefficient (U)= Q/AΛ t

Result:

Average rate of heat transfer was found to be _________ and overall heat transfer

Coefficient was found to be ___________.

Experiment No-3

Aim: To construct drying curve for Calcium Carbonate

Equipment Required: Tray dryer, digital weighing balance, desiccator

Calcium carbonate, anhydrous Calcium chloride

Procedure:

- Take a clean Petridis without lid and determine its weight as w1 g.
- Add 10 grams of Calcium Carbonate to it and weight it as w2 g.
- Add water (10ml) to make a slurry and weigh it as w3 g.
- Keep the dish in tray dryer with temperature maintained at 70C.
- Continue drying and determine the weight of the sample at every 10 minutes after
- Putting it into desiccator containing anhydrous calcium chloride.
- Stop the drying till constant weight is obtained.
- Determine the percentage moisture content and drying rate for each time interval
- Moisture content= w3-w2X100/w3-w1 Drying rate= w3-w2/t2-t1 X w2-w1 h.
- Plot graph between drying rate and moisture content.

Observations and Calculations:

Weight of empty tray = w1 g

Weight of tray with sample = w2 g

Weight of dish with sample and water = w3 g

Moisture content at time 0 minute = w3-w2/ w2-w1

Moisture content after 10 minutes= w4-w2/w2-w1

Result:

The drying rate curve for given sample was plotted. It was observed moisture content _________ with drying

Experiment No. 04

Aim: To study the effect of time on the rate of crystallization.

Required: Beakers, thermometer, ammonic ferric sulphate, water, glass rod, filter paper, funnel, stan

Procedure:

- Take 5 beakers of same size and clean them properly.
- Pour 50 ml of water into all the beakers and heat them till 70oC on a hot plate.
- When the temperature of all the beakers is same, add ammonium ferric sulphate to
- each and stir continuously with help of glass rod.
- Continue the addition and stirring till no more solid is dissolved (super saturated
- solution is formed). e. Keep on stirring for 5 minutes more.
- Place all the beakers in refrigerator at same time.
- Remove one beaker each from refrigerator at 30 minutes interval and filter each
- solution through filter paper.
- Collect the crystals deposited on filter paper and air dry the crystals formed.
- Determine the weight of crystals formed and find the rate of crystallization using the
- formula given below: Rate of crystallization= Weight of crystals formed/ Time
- Draw a graph between time and rate of crystallization.

Observations and Calculations:

s.no	Time in minute	Wight of crystal	Rate of crystallization
1	30		
2	60		
3	90		
4	120		

Result- The rate of crystallization ___________ with time.

Experiment No. 05

AIM: To determine the radiation constant of unpainted glass.

PRINCIPLE: Flow of heat takes place from the high temperature region towards the low temperature region. This is based upon the following three mechanisms.

REQUIREMENTS: Round bottom flask (unpainted) Thermometer (1100) ϖHot plate or burner ϖ Stain with clamp Stop clock, Tripod stand Weighing balance ϖ Purified water

RADIATION:

Mechanism of heat transfer through apace by means of electromagnetic waves is called radiation. A good examples of radiation is black body radiation which occurs by absorbing all energy incidents upon it, at the same time the quantitatively transferred into heat the radiant thermal energy expressed by "STEFFAN BALOZMANN" equation as given below.

$$q = bAT4$$

Where,

q = energy radiated per second

(w) A= Area of radiating surface (m2)

T= absolute temperature of the radiating surface

b= constant w/m2 x k4

Radiation constant is calculated by using following equation,

$M1\ S1 - M2\ S2\ dq/dt = \alpha\ A\ [(T1/100)4 - (T2-100)4\ ] + b\ A\ (T1-T2)$

PROCEDURE:

- A round bottom flask is cleaned and dried
- The weight of the flask is determined(M2/kg)
- The diameter(d) of neck of flask is determined
- Boil hot water is prepared and measured volume of hot water is transferred to the flask (M1). The volume of water is external surface of the round bottom flask is thoroughly dried the flask with hot water is placed on the tripod stand.
- Thermometer (1100) is dipped to centre of the flask and tied at the top to and iron stand.
- Slowly the temperature of the hot body decreases.
- The decrease in temperature is noted every minute.
- The data are recorded in table. A graph is plotted by taking time (minutes) or X-axis and temperature on Y-axis normally is a curve is obtained.

Depending on the temperature at which radiation constant is determined, a tangent is draw

at that temperature the slope is calculated (dq/dt).

Radiation constant (α) is determined at the temperature

Calculations:

Diameter of round bottom flask (d) =

Radius of round bottom flask(r) =

Diameter of neck of round bottom flask (d) =

Radius of neck of round bottom flask (r) =

Surface area of round bottom flask = $4\Pi r2 - \Pi r2$

Empty weight of round bottom flask (M2) =

Volume of heat water with flask (M1) =

Room temperature (t2) =

Derived room temperature (t1) =

Specific heat of water (r1) =

Specific heat of glass (r2) =

$M1\ S1 - M2\ S2\ dq/dt = \alpha A\ [(T1/100)4 - (T2-100)4\ ] + b\ A\ (T1-T2)$

REPORT:

The radiation constant of unpainted glass α =

RESULT-

Experiment No. 06

AIM:- To determine the radiation constant of painted glass.

REQUIREMENT:- Round bottomed painted flask Beaker Thermometer Cork Stand with clamp Stop watch

PRINCIPLE:- Heat transfer by radiation involves the transfer of energy in the form of electromagnetic waves. All solid bodies radiate energy when their temperatures are above absolute zero. The principle form of radiant energy is thermal energy for industrial applications.

The radiant energy emitted by a hot body is expressed by Stefan-Boltzmann law as given below: q= bAT4 Where,

q = Energy radiated per second,

W (or J/s) A = Area of radiating surface,

m2 T = Absolute temperature of the radiating surface, K

B = Constant, W/m2 .K4

The difference in the temperature of hot body and ambient is the temperature gradient for the heat loss by radiation.

The radiation constant (α) is calculated using the following equation:

(M1s1- M2s2) dq/dt = αA [(T1/100)4 - (T1/100)4)] + βA (T1-T2) 1.23

Where, M1 = Mass of water, w g

M2 = Mass of round bottom unpainted flask, kg

S1 = Specific heat of the metal, J/Kg.

S1 = Specific heat of the glass, J/Kg.K (dq/dt) =

Rate of heat loss by metal cylinder, W/s T1 =

Temperature of the metal body, K T2 =

Temperature of the ambient (room temperature), K α =

Radiation constant, W/m2 .K 4 β =

Convection factor A =

Surface area for heat transfer, m2

PROCEDURE:

- 1. Take a round bottom flask, measure the diameter, average radius and then surface area in determined whose heat loss to be calculated

. 2. The Flask neck is covered with a black carbon paper and is hanged in air by tying one end for neck with a thread, and other end to a clamp of stand.

3. Boil the water upto its boiling point and taken in to the flask up to the neck level.

4. The flask is fitted with a rubber cork having one hole, which is fitted with thermometer.

5. The temperature is noted for every 5 min. till it reaches to room temperature.

6. A graph is plotted between temperature on Y-axis and time on X-axis.

7. Calculate the radiation constant.

OBSERVATIONS AND CALCULATIONS:

Time, mins	Temperature, °C	Time, mins	Temperature, °C	Time, mins	Temperature, °C

Weight, M1 =

Diameter of the flask, D =

Radius of the flask, R =

Diameter of the neck, d =

Radius of the neck,r =

Surface area,A =

Surface area of the iron cylinder =

REPORT:-

Experiment No. 07

AIM: -To determine humidity of Air by using Dew point method.

REQUIREMENT:- Round bottom flask having polished surface. Thermometer Tripod Stand Stirrer Humidity Chart

PRINCIPLE: - The Dew point temperature (DPT) is the temperature to which a mixture of air-water vapour must be cool (at constant pressure and constant water vapor content) in order to reach saturation. Formation of mist and disappearance of mist are considered and dew point is determined. Dew point temperature is noted on the temperature axis (x-axis) and moved vertically on the psychrometric chart. The intersect point at saturated curve (100%) is identified. The coordinates of the point (temperature, K, humidity) are noted. The y-axis point is the humidity of air. These values are substituted in the equation.

Percent relative humidity= (humidity of air/ humidity of saturated air) X 100

PROCEDURE:-

- Take a polished round bottom flask (100 ml) and fill water upto 2/3 of its volume
- Place the flask on tripod stand and fix it.
- . Hang a thermometer hanging from the main stand such that the thermometer's bulb is dipping into the water in the vessel
- Drop small pieces of ice cubes into the vessel one by one slowly, under continuous stirring of the water with the help of glass rod or magnetic stirrer.
- Continue the stirring until a film of moisture (mist) is firmed on the polished surface of flask.
- Note the temperature of this stage which is dew point and record it. 6. Denote humidity of air by using dew point with the help of humidity.

OBSERVATION AND CALCULATION:-

s.no of trail	Dew point		Humidity

REPORT:-

Experiment No. 08

AIM: Description of Construction Working and application of Pharmaceutical machinery Such as Rotary Tablet Machine, Fluidized Bed Coated, Fluid Energy Mill, Dehumidifier.

1) ROTARY TABLET MACHINE: It is also called multi station tablet press. It is called rotary machine rotary machine because the head of the machine that holds the upper punches, dies and lower punches in place rotates

Steps involved in manufacturing of tablet:

- The material to fed through hopper
- The fill cam pulls the lower punches down to a fixed distance and the dies are filled with material •
- The quantity of the material filled is larger than the actual amount required,
- remove excess amount with the help of spatula
- After that, upper punch is lowered and inserted into the dies
- The material is compressed and the tablet are formed
- After the compression, pulls the upper punches into their top position and simultaneously lift the lower punches until the tablets are ejected from the dies
- Then the tablet is passed through discharge chute

Applications: ¬

- It is operated continuously
- Used for large scale production
- A single rotary press produce 1150 tablets in a minute while double rotary press can produce 10,000 tablets in a minute

2) FLUIDIZED BED COATER: Three types of air suspension coater are available, namely top spray coater, wurster or bottom spray coater, and tangential spray coater. In top spray coater, there is a counter current (opposite position) it movement of powder particles or pellets and liquid spray. In wurster or bottom spray coater, there is a concurrent (same direction) movement of powder particles or pellets and liquid spray. In tangential spray coater, the powder particles or pellets move in a helical fashion due to spinning rotor disk on the bottom of the equipment.

Steps involved in wurster or bottom spray coater:

- The drying inlet air is passed upwards through the bottom perforated plate into the fluid bed chamber This air passes to wurster column, in which a spray gun perpendicular to bottom plate and parallel to the wurster column
- This air passes out from the exhaust filters situated at the top of the equipment
- The material to be coated is located is loaded in the fluid bed chamber and fluidized

Application:

- It is used to coat pharmaceutical dosage form with polymeric material to mark objectionable taste or odour and also to protect an unstable ingredient and to improve appearance
- Fluidized bed coaters are used for coating of powders, granules, tablets, pellets etc by column of air
- Fluidized bed coating equipment is popular for coating multiparticulate systems such as beads and non parallel seeds

FLUID ENERGY MILL:

- A fluid usually air is injected at very high pressure through nozzles at the bottom of the loop, as a result turbulence produce ϖ Solids are introduced into the steam through hopper
- Due to this turbulence occur and impacts and attrition occur between the particles
- A classifier is fitted at the exist so that only finer size particles are collected as products
- The larger size particles are again sent to the stream of air for further size reduction
- Application:
- The particle size of the product is smaller when compared to other method of size reduction
- No chance of contamination of the product
- This material is suitable where fine powders are required like micro ionization or griseofulvin

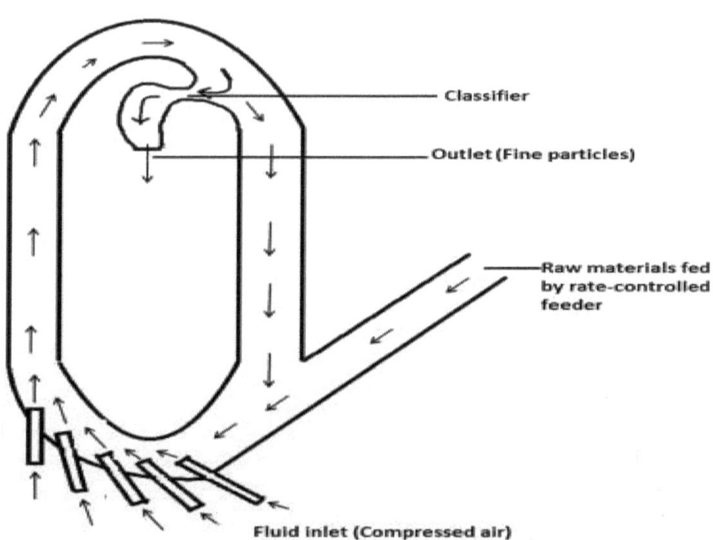

3) DE-HUMIDIFIER:

- Warm moist air is sucked in through one side of the machine
- An electric fan is used to draws the air inward
- The warm air passes through cold pipes through which a coolant circulators, due to cooling of air, the moisture it contains turns back into liquid water
- Then the air passes over a heating element and warms back up to its original temperature Warm, dry air blows back into the room through another side of machine
- The moisture that was in the air drips down into a collecting tray at the bottom of the machine As the collecting tray fills up, a plastic float in the machine rises upward
- When the tray is fill, the float trips an electric switch that turns off the fan and switches on an indicator light which indicates that the machine needs emptying
- Applications:
- A dehumidifier is used to reduce the levels of humidity in the air
- Large dehumidifier are used in commercial buildings such as indoor ice rinks to control the humidity level

RESULT-

Experiment No. 09

AIM: Demonstrating Colloid Mill, Planetary Mixer, Fluidized Bed Dryer, .

- COLLOID MILL:
  - The colloid mill used to reduce the size of the suspended droplets
  - The material is feed in through the inlet hopper and placed into the mill
  - It is then move through the narrow gap between the rotor and stator to reduce the particle size
  - Then final product is removed through the outlet

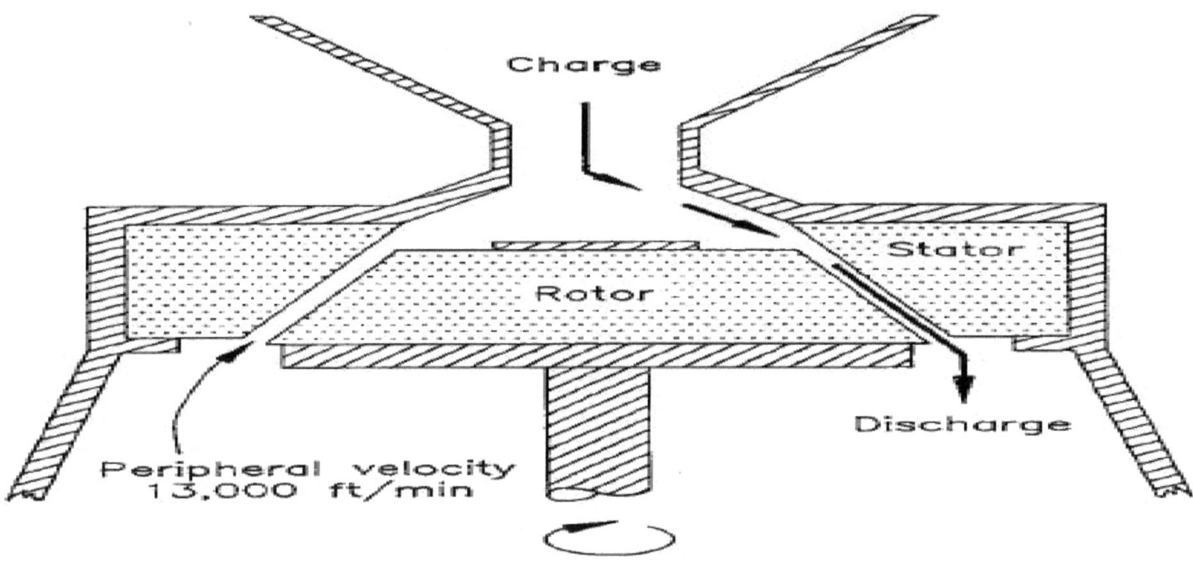

2) PLANETARY MIXER:

- The material to be mixed is loaded into mixing bowl or shell
- The blades rotate on their own axis when they orbit the mixing bowl on a common axis.
- Therefore there is no dead spot in the mixing and high shear is applied for mixing
- After mixing, the material is discharged through a bottom value or by manual scooping of the material from the bowl

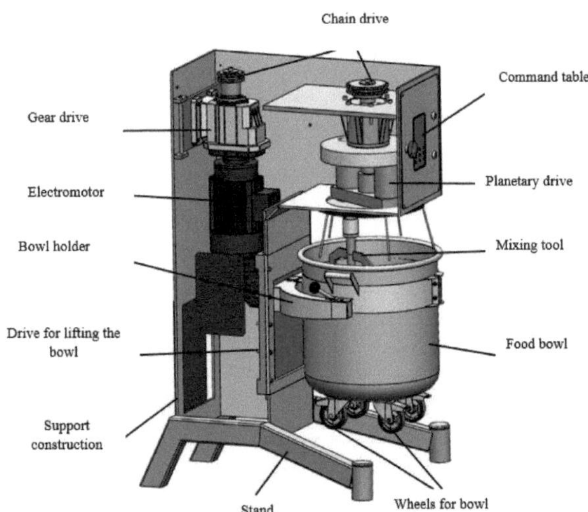

FLUIDIZED BED DRYER:

- The wet granules to be dried are placed in a detachable bowl, the bowl is inserted in the dryer
- Fresh air can pass through a pre filter, which is then heated when passing through a heat exchanger
- Hot air flows through the bottom of the bowl at the same times, the fan starts to rotate the air speed increases gradually
- After a specific time a pressure point is reached in which the friction drag on the particles is equal to the force of gravity. The granules rise in the container. This condition is said to be fluidized state
- The gas surrounds each granule to dry them completely the air comes out of the dryer passing through the filters in the bag
- The entrained particles remain adhered to the interior of the surface of the bags. Periodically, the bags are shaken to remove entrained particles
- The materials are left in the dryer to reach room temperature
- The bowl is removed, the final product is free flowing

Experiment No. 10

Aim: To study the effect of various factors on the rate of filtration

Equipment Required: funnel, digital weighing balance

Material Required: Calcium Carbonate, water, beaker, measuring cylinder, volumetric flask, glass rod, Whatman filter paper.

Theory:

Filtration is any of various mechanical and physical operation that separates solid from liquid through a media by which the liquid can pass. Rate of filtration is affected by viscosity, thickness of filter bed, temperature, area and pressure.

Procedure:

a. Prepare 50 ml each of 1 %w/v, 5% w/v and 10% w/v of Calcium Carbonate slurry.

b. Set the filtration assembly using Whatman filter paper and pour the slurry over the funnel for filtration.

c. Note down the volume of filtrate obtained after every 30 seconds till entire amount has been filtered

d. Calculate rate of filtration at each time interval by using the formula given below.

Rate of filtration= Amount of filtrate/ Time of filtration

e. Repeat the process for other concentration of $CaCO_3$ slurry.

f. Plot the graph by taking concentration on x-axis and time of filtration on y-axis.

Observations and Calculations:

S.NO	TIME IN SECOND	VOLUME OF FILTRATION	RATE OF FILTRATION
1			
2			
3			
4			

Result:

Rate of filtration_____________ with increase in thickness of filter cake.

Experiment No.11

AIM: To study the effect of time on the rate of crystallization.

REQUIREMENTS: Beakers Slide Cover slip Microscope

PROCEDURE:

Refined bleached and deodorized palm oil are placed in a beaker which was initially heated in a thermally controlled water bath for 30 minutes at 70ºC to totally melt the oil .

The temperature was then reduced to 30ºC within one hour followed by reducing to crystallization temperature of 14 or 22ºC within 30 minutes. Once the oil reached the desired temperature (14 or 22ºC), it was allowed to crystallize until 90 minutes where the analyses were made at 5,15,30,60 and 90 minutes to obtain the morphology of the crysta

The beaker content was constantly stirred at 90 rpm throughout the process using a stirring motor attached with two blades paddle propeller Samples of slurries were withdrawn at 5,15,30,60 and 90 minutes of crystallization and placed onto a slide which was then covered with a cover slip.

Photograph of the crystals were taken at the magnification of 200x The lengths of four longest dimensions of each crystal were recorded and an average of at least six crystals was measured during each observation.

Observation table:

Time (min)	Crystal Size (μm)

Report: Rate of crystallization of palm oil---------------------------

Experiment No.12

Aim: To calculate the mixing index for given sample by using Double Cone Blender.

Equipment Required: Double Cone blender, Digital weighing balance

Material Required: Burette, burette stand, conical flask, sample scoop, talc, Calcium carbonate, phenolphthalein, Hydrochloric acid, oxalic acid, sodium hydroxide

Theory:

Double cone blender is used for solid-solid mixing. The symmetry in the mixer is disturbed by putting barriers acting as baffles. Mixing is due to shearing action. It is used for small amounts of powder.

Procedure:

a. Weigh 500 g of talc and 500g of calcium carbonate separately.

b. Mix talc and Calcium carbonate using double cone blender. Run the equipment for 30 minutes.

c. Withdraw 100 mg of sample from different places of mixer. Take 20 such samples.

d. Place the samples separately in 20 conical flasks each containing 30 ml of 0.1 N HCl .

e. Shake the contents of the flask thoroughly to complete the reaction between HCl and Calcium Carbonate.

f. Determine the unreacted acid by titrating against 0.1 N solution of standardised sodium hydroxide solution using phenolphthalein as indicator.

g. Standardisation of NaOH was done using 0.1 N Oxalic acid.

h. Determine the conversion factor and find the mixing index.

Observations and Calculations:

Vol of sodium hydroxide consumed= …….ml(x)

A mixture of 100mg of calcium carbonate and 30 ml of HCl consumes xml of ….N NaOH solution. Therefore, Unreacted HCl in the vessel reacted with xml of sodiumhydroxide solution.

Normality of sodium hydroxide solution (N2) = …….N

Vol of sodium hydroxide solution = x = …….ml

Normality of hydrochloric acid solution (N3) = …….NEq.

vol. of HCl unreacted (e)=(N2) × (x) / N3 ………ml (30 – e) ml of HCl reacts with 100mg of calcium carbonate

1ml of HCl reacts with 100/(30-e)= [c mg] of calcium carbonate c/1000 =……..g of calcium carbonate (d) d = Eq. factor

OBSERVATION TABLE

S.NO	Volume of NaOH	Volume of HCl reacted with CaCO3(A)= 30 – volume of HCl consumed	Weight of CaCO3(y)=AXd	y-x, where x is amount of mixed sample w.r.t total amouT	(y-x)2

Mixing index=√Σ(y-x)2 /n

Result: The mixing index was found to be__________

Experiment No.13

Aim: To evaluate size distribution of tablet granulations/ powder by sieve analysis and construct various size frequency curves including arithmetic and logarithmic probability plots.

.Materials Required: Calcium Carbonate/ granules

Theory:

Sieve analysis is the size separation method used in determining the average particle size of a given powder. Powder is made to pass through a set of standard sieves which are arranged in ascending order of the sieve number. The sieve shaker subjects this powder to different types of agitation so that size separation occurs rapidly. Standard sieves as per Pharmacopoeia where in sieve mesh size , number, diameter of wire used , aperture tolerance is specified.

Procedure:

a. Arrange the set of sieves in the descending order.

b. Weighed 10 grams of sample and place it in sieve at the top of the sieve set.

c. Start the sieving shaker. The length of time and speed of vibration can be controlled by semiautomatic or automatic attachment in the machine.

d. Collect the powder material retained on the various sieves and in pan. Weigh the powdered material retained on the sieves.

f. Calculate percent frequency of each size of particle and plot the graphs.

g. Determine the geometric mean weight diameter and geometrical standard deviation

h. Plot frequency distribution curves (undersize, oversize), arithmetic and logarithmic probability plot

Observations and Calculations

S.NO	Sieve no. passed/ retained	Arthmetic mean opening (μ)	Weight retained on sieve (g)	Cumulative weight retained on sieve (g)	Cumulative % weight retained (%)	Arithmetic mean opening (μ	Cumulative Weight retained undersize (g)	Cumulative % weight retained undersize(%)

Result:

Size distribution frequency curves including arithmetic and logarithmic probability graphs were plotted.

Printed by Libri Plureos GmbH in Hamburg,
Germany